DO YOU WANT TO SEE YOUR FUTURE?

Let the magic begin...

JANET LAKE

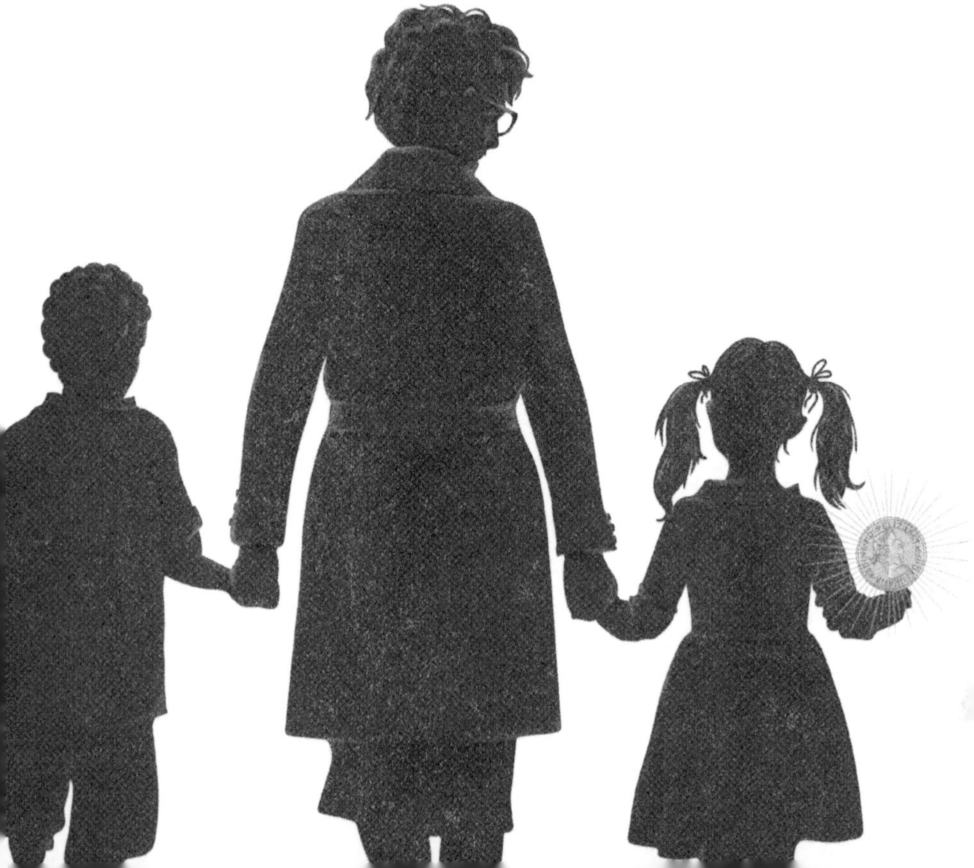

DO YOU WANT TO SEE YOUR FUTURE?

Let the magic begin...

JANET LAKE

ELE BOOKS

This is a work of fiction. Names, characters, places, and incidents either are the product of the author's imagination or are used fictitiously. Any resemblance to actual persons, living or dead, events, or locales is entirely coincidental.

Copyright © 2024 by Janet M. Lake

All rights reserved. No part of this book may be reproduced or used in any manner without written permission of the copyright owner except for the use of quotations in a book review.

First published in 2024

Edited by Alex Chapman
Designed by Clare Baggaley

ISBN 979 8338171 36 3 (paperback)

This book is a dedication to my mother, who sadly passed away a few years ago. She inspired me by writing a book herself about a magic ring. Although my sister and I thought the story was very good, she never did anything about getting it published, which was a shame.

I was thinking about this during the Covid shutdown period, when the idea came to me that I could write a similar story for children about a magic penny that could help and educate them as well as being interesting and fun.

DEI·GRATIA·REGINA·F:D:
BOURBON
F:D: ✝ELIZABETH·II·DEI·GRATIA
ONE PENNY
1967
ONE

CONTENTS

CHAPTER ONE page 9

CHAPTER TWO page 19

CHAPTER THREE page 25

CHAPTER FOUR page 31

CHAPTER FIVE page 43

CHAPTER SIX page 51

CHAPTER SEVEN page 59

CHAPTER EIGHT page 67

CHAPTER NINE page 73

CHAPTER TEN page 81

CHAPTER ELEVEN page 89

CHAPTER TWELVE page 97

ABOUT THE AUTHOR page 100

CHAPTER ONE

BOOM, RUMBLE, CRACK, BANG

From above, the sky was making the most awful noises. However, the sun at present was still peeping through the grey clouds. It was a late September afternoon, Mrs Joyce Hill, her daughter Susy and her son Jake were walking into the little village of Westernmere, which was a quiet village some way away from the main town of Eastenbrook.

"Are we going to the sweet shop?" asked Susy who was 7 years old. "Are we going to the toy shop?" asked Jake who was 9 years old and thought himself much more grown up than his younger sister. "I think I would rather get way from all these noises" Susy said in rather timid voice.

"We are not going to either I'm afraid" replied their mother, "I have to make an important visit to the Westernmere Bank today. We must get there before this storm breaks." As they arrived at the door of the bank their mother said to the children, "I must talk to the nice gentleman Manager of the bank Mr Hodgson, so I want you both to be very quiet and behave and then there might be a little reward for you when I have finished."

Susy and Jake sat on a bench waiting, both swinging their legs, funnily in time with each other. "This is a strange old building" said Susy, looking up at the high ceiling and then at the old wood panelling, "I must ask Mum if it was a house or something else before it was a bank" Jake was not interested in the bank, he asked, "I wonder what reward we will get when Mum has finished, I hope it is ice-cream or maybe even a toy from the toy shop"

Meanwhile, Mrs Hill sat in the Bank Manager's office in a worn leather chair, looking around and just like her daughter wondering about the old wood panelling and Mr Hodgson's large old desk, but not bothering to ask about it, as she had more important things on her mind.

Mr Hodgson was an overweight, red-faced man, but had a kindly smiley face normally, but today he was looking rather serious, he sat back in his old leather chair, which looked like something out of Dickens, but at odds with the modern equipment on the desk. "I was very sorry to hear about your husband Mrs Hill, it must have been an awful

CHAPTER ONE

shock him dying so suddenly like that. Sometimes heart problems go undetected, and the poor heart just gives out and stops."

"Thank you, Mr Hodgson, yes it was a terrible shock and I miss Norman dreadfully, but what has happened has made the shock even worse, we don't seem to have hardly any money in the bank, which is why I rang you and asked to come in today." Mrs Hill took out a beautiful white embroidered handkerchief and dabbed at her eyes.

Mr Hodgson waited a while until Mrs Hill had composed herself and then spoke quietly and seriously to her, "Mrs Hill I have some bad news and some good news for you; the bad is that unfortunately your husband made some very bad investments and lost a lot of his money; the good news is that at last his life insurance has been paid out. After paying off a few small debts and his funeral costs there is not a lot left I am afraid, but what there is should keep you and your family financially secure for the time being."

Mrs Hill left the office feeling a little happier about her circumstances, than she had in a while. Now the bills could be paid, and they had enough to be comfortable for at least the current time, but what would happen after that?

The children jumped up and ran to meet their mother, Susy hugged her, but Jake complained that she had been such a long time, then asked "what was their reward as they had both been particularly good." Their mother said "because I was longer than I expected we will not be able to go anywhere today as we have to get home and if you look outside, you can now see some very black clouds, so I think it is going to pour with rain any time." She grabbed both children's hands and started to walk briskly along the pavement towards home, as many other residents of Westernmere were doing, anticipating the storm.

Susy sighed as she was rushed past the sweet shop, but Jake started to pull on his mother's hand "I want to go in and look at the toys Mum," he cried," not today Jake" his mother replied, "we must get home now."

They arrived home just as the first large spots of rain started to fall and the thunder and lightning were deafening, they rushed towards the front door. Susy was always pleased that their front door was a lovely shiny red colour, compared to the dull brown, grey and dark green of the other houses in the street, she thought No 20 Jamesmoor Road had the best-looking door and the nicest small front patio, that even at this time of year was covered in pots with geraniums, ivys and small fir trees. Her mother liked to keep it tidy and as colourful as possible.

Once inside, Jake was still sulking about not being allowed to visit the toy shop. Mrs Hill felt a little guilty, as she had promised them a reward if they

CHAPTER ONE

were good, which they had been in the bank. She called them both to her, "sorry about rushing you home, but I am expecting a phone call from your Aunt Della, so I do have to get back, however, I did draw out some money while I was at the bank, so I can give you some extra pocket money for you to spend when we next go out." Mrs Hill opened her handbag and then her purse and gave both a large handful of coins. "Look how they are all new and shiny" she said.

The children were delighted to see an assortment of coins from pennies to half-crowns, all of them new and sparkling. Just then the phone rang, and Mrs Hill dashed off to answer it, as it was probably her sister Della.

Susy had picked up one of the shiny pennies to look closely at it, but she nearly dropped it again; a small young voice said "Hello nice to meet you." Both her and Jake looked round to see who was speaking. "Hello, yes it is me" said the coin, "you are the first people I have spoken to since I left the Royal Mint" the children looked at the coin in amazement. "Are you a magic penny?" said Jake. "I am not sure what I am" said the coin, "but I have been given an important job to do from a senior coin at the Royal Mint, let me try to explain to you."

DO YOU WANT TO KNOW YOUR FUTURE?

*"I can tell you horrors or sorrows,
　could be today or might be tomorrow.
It could bring you joy or terrible tears,
　it maybe in days or sometimes in years.
It might be your fate, but it is never too late,
　change your ways now to make things right.
Don't be bad and go to the dark,
　I can help you see back to the light."*

Both children looked at each, with a puzzled expression on their faces, "we don't understand," said Jake. "I am sorry" said the penny, " it was what was told to me at the Royal Mint." "What is the Royal Mint" asked Susy. "Ah that I can explain said the penny, this is what I learnt, and you can learn it too."

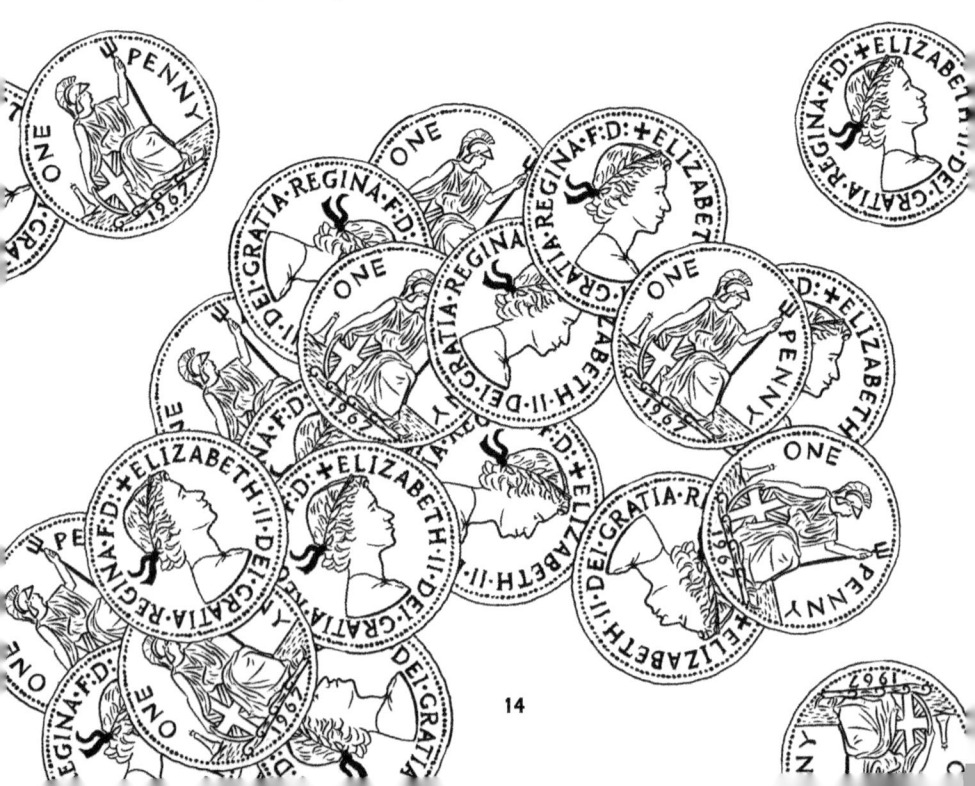

CHAPTER ONE

- **THE ROYAL MINT, LONDON** – owned by Her Majesty's Treasury, produces all coins, medals and bullion. Each coin denomination is made from an alloy, which is a mixture of metals.
- The rolling mill makes the metal hard, so it must be softened, to do this, it must be treated in temperatures of up to 950° centigrade (that is extremely hot.)
- A strip is passed through powerful rolling mills that reduce it down to the thickness of a coin. Discs of the metal are then punched from the strip by a blanking press. The press can make up to 10,000 discs (called blanks) per minute.
- The blanks are then cleaned to make sure there are no marks or blemishes.
- An engraving machine then uses a digital file to cut the design into a piece of steel that is the size of the of the final coin. The final part of the process is the blanks are fed into a coining press that a pair of dies (a device used to cut chosen shapes) it applies a pressure of around 60 tonnes, the dies strike the blanks and turns them into coins at a speed of 850 strikes per minute.
- A 3D pattern is now viable. The new shiny coins are then bagged and sent to storage before distribution – this is usually to banks.

The penny hoped the children were not too young to understand about the Royal Mint, but it was Susy who asked the next question – "it still does not explain how you can talk to us in our heads" she said, "and why?" "You say you can tell us our fate, which would be interesting to hear" but Susy also being the most practical – even for her age also said "and why have you not got a proper name; we can't just keep calling you penny?" "I will tell you my instructions from the Royal Mint first and then we will think about names"

"This was my command" -

> *"Go into this world and do your best,*
> *I will tell you how and you do the rest.*
> *I am the oldest coin, so do not be dense,*
> *and listen to this old six pence.*
> *What you can do is extra special, looking into the future for what may be, you have the ability to make them change what they might see.*
> *You are new, clean and bright, you can help people change so life is good and right."*

That is all that I was told by an old ancient looking six pence piece before I was put in a bag and sent off to the bank where your mother picked me up. As for a name I do not have one, so, you can give me one if you like. Both Susy and Jake started to shout out names, like Jane and Jill, and Tom and John, but then Jake said," you seem to like rhymes a lot, so maybe you need a name that rhymes with penny; I know" said Susy "in a book I was reading, there was a bear called Benny, that name rhymes with penny" for once Jake and Susy agreed, that

CHAPTER ONE

it was a very suitable name.

"Yes" said the penny, "I think I like that name; you may call me Benny in the future."

CHAPTER TWO

The penny, or Benny as the children now called him had been with the children a few weeks, he had asked them not to tell their mother about him for the time being as he needed to think about what his place was in this family he had found himself in. Susy and Jake were becoming a little bored with him to be honest, they thought a magic penny would be far more interesting and do lots of exciting things, but that had not happened so far.

The children's autumn half term break was finished, and they were now back at school. Mrs Hill had been to the school to pick up Susy and had found her to be very quiet and not looking at all happy. "What is wrong with you today" asked her mother, "you do not seem to be your usual self, are you having trouble with your class work? Has the teacher been telling you off?"

"No there is nothing wrong" said Susy in a small voice, "I am alright". Mrs Hill was still a bit worried, but she thought she would let it go for now.

When they got home, Mrs Hill said "go and change out of your school uniform Susy before you go and play." Susy did not need telling twice; although she quite liked the navy and white check dresses and the navy blazer with the light blue edging that was the school uniform, she still preferred to get into a pair of jeans and sweatshirt later.

Susy went to her bedroom and changed, still looking a bit down, she picked up the small box (an old jewellery box she had been given, with different coloured painted shells on the top) that they kept Benny in and took him out.

"Well, you are not looking very happy today" said Benny, "what is the problem?" Susy had been reluctant to tell her mother, but she thought it would do no harm to tell Benny – well he was only a penny after all. "The girls in my class keep teasing me because we are not as well off as them. They say I have not got nice clothes like them, or many toys. They say we have not got a car or even bikes like they have. They make me cry when they say I have not got a Dad like they have, and that he died because he was ashamed of his own family," sniffed Susy. "Today they took my sandwiches away from me and laughed that we

CHAPTER TWO

could not even afford school dinners."

"That is not right, that is bullying" said Benny, "you need to tell your mother what is happening and your teacher. "Oh, I couldn't" cried Susy, "that would make matters worse."

Benny said:
*"I understand fully it is not good to be bullied,
   but I tell you once and even twice it is so
   much better to be nice.
But if you just let it go, bad habits will begin to show,
   it will lead to loss and lots of distress.
It would be awfully sad, if you also turned bad,
   don't let your mind get in a whirl, because
   I think you are a really nice girl."*

Then all of a sudden there was a long whistle and a loud bang, and a bright light, and a hole like the beginning of a tunnel appeared. Somehow through some instinct Benny knew what it was – "this is showing you your future, your fate, you need to look into the hole to see it."

Susy was quite frightened, it sounded like the storm all over again, but she was also intrigued as to what she would see, she slowly moved forward to peer into the hole and then nearly jumped back again, when she saw herself, but looking a lot different. She looked to be about 16 or 17 years of age, taller and with longer hair. She was standing in front of some younger girls and shouting at them, saying they were useless, and that their schoolwork was no good and they might as well throw their books away, or she would do it for them. She then told them to hand over their pocket money and their dinner money to her. She advised them that if they told anyone, she would come and sort each one of them out.

Susy stood there looking shocked, "what was that all about" she asked Benny, "that can't have been me, I would never do anything like that."

"I think at last I see what my role here is, and I understand the rhyme that came to me. This is the future as it could be. I know that people who have been bullied and not done anything to put it right, often go on to be even bigger bullies themselves. This is a warning to you Susy, that you must tell someone, like your mum or teacher, or it will only get worse, and you might end up like that future self you have just seen."

"I will do" cried Susy," can I tell my mum what you did to make me need to tell someone about the bullying?" Benny looked thoughtful, "I am going against what I just said, but I would rather you did not tell your mother about me at the moment. First because she may not believe you and then it might make it difficult for her to believe you about the

CHAPTER TWO

bullying and secondly, I am not sure about what I am supposed to do or say in front of adults; you accept me because you are young, but I don't know what the circumstances would be if you told an older person. Sorry to have to ask but can you keep it between us for now."

Susy nodded, "I sort of understand, it is a bit like us believing in Father Christmas, elves and the tooth fairy, but for some reason adults don't."

Susy then went off to find her mother to tell her the rather sad story of her bullying, it was going to be hard, but now she knew she was doing the right thing.

The next afternoon when Susy came home from school she had her mother with her, she was still noticeably quiet, but she did look happier than the previous day. After she had changed out of her school uniform and her mother had given her a glass of milk and a biscuit, telling her she had been a good and brave girl, she ran to find Benny. "It was hard telling the head teacher, but having mum sitting with me was better. Miss McDonald was truly kind and said she would not have that sort of behaviour going on in her school. She is going to see all the girls involved and advise them that it must stop; she will be advising their mothers about it and she will be keeping an eye on the girls. If she sees it happening again, or I tell her that they have been bullying me again; she will take very serious steps to see that they are punished and could even be expelled from the school."

"Well, I hope they have learnt a lesson and that you have too young Susy." "Oh, I have" said Susy, "and thank you so much Benny you are a good friend to me, and I will never think of you as just a penny again" Susy bought Benny up to her lips and gave him a big kiss. Benny did not know what to think of this, but thought if he were not made of metal, he was sure he would have blushed.

CHAPTER THREE

A few days later, Benny was quite surprised when Jake suddenly opened the box he was in and snatched him up. Jake was in Susy's pretty pink and white bedroom, with old fashioned but still nice wallpaper with pink rosebuds on it and a bed cover with pink rabbits on (which he had heard Susy say was now a bit babyish for her, but secretly she still loved it.)

"Now" said Jake, "if you are a magic penny, I want you to make this money I have collected here in my hand, into a lot more. I want to be able to buy the train set I have seen in the toy shop window, but mum says it is too expensive and she cannot afford to buy it for me."

Benny said sadly; "I am really sorry Jake, that is not the sort of magic I can do, it is not possible for me." "Well what good are you to me then" replied Jake angrily, "I will just have to get the money elsewhere"

Benny was dismayed to see Jake looking around the room and then peering out of the lounge door, before going over to the shelf by the fireplace and picking up his mother's handbag and taking out her purse. He looked through it until he saw some notes in the back pocket and took them out.

Benny Said:
> *"Really think how bad we'll feel, if you are going to start to steal, I don't want the belief you will become a horrid thief.*
> *Think of your mother when she sees you rob, she will surely start to cry and sob. Do you think it is fine to do this crime you really are crossing a dangerous line. Your life will fail, and you'll get caught and it will end with you being in jail?*
> *The police will take you and there will be no release, life would be hell inside a cell.*
> *Now is the time for your path to pick, or you will find yourself in the nick."*

Then suddenly there was a whistle, a loud bang, a bright light, and a hole like the beginning of a tunnel appeared. Oh, thought Benny I have seen this before, this is another telling of the future!

Jake stood his eyes wide open; he shook his head

CHAPTER THREE

and could not believe what was happening, he peered through the hole and in even more disbelief, he saw himself, but looking older than he was now.

"Right" said Benny "this is the lesson you must learn." These are the words Jake heard;

- What used to be named **BORSTAL JUVENILE DETENTION REFORM SYSTEM** in Kent, opened in 1902. It was intended to separate young offenders from the influence of older hardened criminals and provide then with education and training
- In 1902 the boys were made to work; in fields, doing gardening, on buildings as brick layers or carpenters, and even in an iron foundry.
- They had to do exercises in a yard in all weathers. The Guards were big burly men who were often cruel.
- The boys had a small room on their own (if they were lucky) or slept in a dormitory with others, both had wooden floors and no heating.
- To be sent there, if you went to court for stealing the judge could sentence anyone between the ages of 12 to 17 a custodial sentence of 4 month to 2 years.
- If it were a more serious crime or you re-offended, they would-be put-on remand and a Youth Justice board decided which secure centre a young person would be sent to, suitable for their age, sex, background and again if you were lucky somewhere near your home.
- In 1982 it was replaced by institutions called Young Offender Institutions (for 15-17 year olds – called Juvenile offenders)

DO YOU WANT TO KNOW YOUR FUTURE?

> plus an 18 to 20 year olds institute.
> - When you arrive at the place of custody in these days, the conditions will be a bit better, but still as strict. You will have your belongs taken away from you, including money, keys, and your phone, and you will be stripped searched to ensure you don't have drugs on you.
> - You will meet your personal officer who will allocate your training program for learning skills, participating in sport and the work you will carry out. You will be advised of family visiting times (you are not allowed visits outside of these times, which are usually once a week.)

Jake looked back in the hole and saw the Young Offenders Institute which looked grim and saw his older self, looking incredibly sad and lonely, sitting on a small single bed, with no home comforts and no family around him; then in a room packing boxes for hours on end. The scene changes and he saw himself even older in a prison cell, with guards outside and lots of noise from all the other men, then a guard said you only have another 10 years to be in here Jake!

Then just as suddenly the hole/tunnel shut down, and it was as if it had never been there.

"NO, NO!" cried Jake. Looking as white as a sheet," I don't want to end up in that special school or in prison and not be with or see my mum and sister and I would want my dad to be proud of me,

CHAPTER THREE

not ashamed. Will that really happen to me in the future" " It does not have to" said Benny, "it depends on how you behave. Stealing from your own mother, when she does not have a lot of money, is bad enough, but once you do that and get away with it you may go on to think that is ok and look to where else you can obtain things, like shop lifting, or stealing from friends, it is a slippery slope Jake and what your saw could be what happens to you, if you do not mend your ways now."

"I do not want to end up like that" cried Jake, looking very agitated, he picked up the money he had taken from his mother's purse, plus the other money that was originally his own pocket money and ran and put it all into his mother's purse. "I will never do that again," he said, "and I will not worry mum for things she cannot afford either. I will also appreciate my sister more."

"I knew you were a good boy at heart" said Benny, "and now you have learnt a valuable lesson of what could have happened to you in the future, I am sure you will always remember to be honest." "Thank you" replied Jake, "I am not sure how you did that, but I am grateful, now I will put you back in your box so that you can have a rest."

CHAPTER FOUR

Joyce Hill is sitting in her lounge in the early afternoon, she looks around her, the furniture, the carpet, and curtains are quite old (in fact quite old fashioned she thinks) but not too shabby and all certainly clean. She then looks down at herself, she has dressed smartly (certainly not her absolute best clothes) but ones she keeps when she goes visiting or is expecting visitors. A smart grey skirt, a crisp white blouse, and a green jacket (that she thinks of as a Robin Hood colour).

She has made a bit of an effort with her hair today, washed this morning and blow-dried carefully. She also has a little make-up on, which she does not usually wear unless she is going out. She is also looking a little apprehensive. The children are at school, which is just as well as they would be asking her all sorts of questions.

Joyce is not going out, but she is expecting a visitor, she had a phone call the day before from her husband Norman's old boss of Bolden Computers; Peter Westbrook. Peter had been a good friend of Norman and been to dinner at the house many times. When he phoned he had asked Joyce if he could come round and see her this afternoon as he had something important to discuss with her. Joyce had never seen Peter on her own before and certainly could not think what he wanted to talk to her about. Peter lived in the biggest house in Westernmere, called Westernmere Manor.

Suddenly Joyce was bought back from her thoughts, by the doorbell ringing, she jumped up to answer it. She was surprised to see Peter on the doorstep with a large bunch of beautiful flowers, carnations, daisies, and beautiful roses, which were her favourites. "Do come in" said Joyce standing aside to let him in, "what lovely flowers', "they are for you" said Peter, looking a little embarrassed, "I bought them to cheer you up and to say again how sorry I am about Norman, we miss him at work, but I am sure you miss him so much more. How are you and the children coping?" Joyce was not sure what to say – "well it has been extremely hard without Norman and yes of course we miss him terribly. I am glad to say the children have been coping well with their loss." "Do come and sit down,

CHAPTER FOUR

while I put these flowers in water and put the kettle on, would you like tea or coffee, or perhaps you would like something stronger? I think Norman had a bottle of scotch somewhere." "No, a cup of tea would be lovely" said Pete, "can I give you a hand with anything?" "No, I can manage, you just sit down and relax."

Joyce bought out a tray with tea, milk and sugar, and a plate of biscuits and put it on the coffee table. "This is a nice quaint and homely room," said Pete. *(What he really means is old fashioned and worn, like I was thinking earlier, thought Joyce)* but she just replied, "thank you Peter."

After drinking his tea and having a biscuit, Peter said "I had better let you know why I have come round this afternoon. I have two things I want to discuss with you. Firstly let me tell you that Norman discussed with me before he died about how he had made a terrible mistake in some investments, and lost a lot of money, and how he did not know how he was going to tell you, but he was going to do that and was going to try and make it right. Unfortunately, he just didn't get the time. I therefore know that things money wise must be exceedingly difficult for you. I have always admired you and Norman and how good you were together, and Norman was a good friend to me when my father also died suddenly. Therefore, I want to help you" Joyce was shaking her head, "you are very kind, but I cannot take any money help from you, it would not be right."

"I know you would be too proud to take any charitable offer, so I have come up with a plan; I know before you had the children that you used to be a Manager of a publishing firm, so you have many office skills, I want to offer you a job, nothing too complicated, but I need some reports typed up and some accounts work, which I can show you how to do. I realise the children need to be considered so perhaps you could do some of the work at home, and just come into the office sometimes while the children are at school.

"I will need time to think about it" replied Joyce "but it does seem to be the answer to my prayers regarding our finances." "I understand" said Peter," you think about it and then let me know, and if you decide yes – which I hope you will, we can make some arrangements." "Thank you," said Joyce "it is very kind of you to think of me, and I will let you know soon. You said there were two things you want to talk to me about what was the other thing?"

Peter looked down at his shoes, which were very smart and expensive, and then looked up at Joyce. "I think this is the one that is more difficult to talk to you about" he said. Joyce looked apprehensive; "perhaps you had better just tell me."

"Well, we are having a Company dinner dance at the weekend being held in the hall at my manor,

CHAPTER FOUR

and as you know I have no partner to be with me, I wondered if you would do me the honour of being with me? I know what you are going to say, that it is too soon after Norman's death, but I know he would not want you to be sad all the time and not getting out of the house for any enjoyment. I believe you have known how I felt about you for some time, I think you are a wonderful woman. I would never have done anything about it while Norman was alive, and neither would you, I thought too much of both of you, but what do you say about coming to the dinner dance night with me, just as friends, well for now, he said smiling with a glint in his eyes?"

Joyce looked panicked, and stammered "I just don't know, I have many things to consider, including if I can get a babysitter and what I would wear." Ok said Peter I will leave you both of my suggestions to consider, but the dinner one I would like to know tomorrow if you could."

Peter stood up, pulled at the creases in his smart navy suit and said his goodbyes, giving Joyce a peck on the cheek. He would always do this when he came to dinner before, but she thought if felt different this time.

Joyce had to then rush off to collect the children from school, but her mind was all over the place thinking about the decisions she had to make.

She made the children's dinner of chicken pie,

potatoes, and green beans, but she was still in rather a dream. "Are you alright mum" asked Susy, "you do not seem yourself, I see you had a visitor this afternoon, as there were two cups and saucers in the drainer on the sink"

Trust Susy thought Joyce, she does not miss anything. "I had your dad's old boss round, you remember Peter, don't you? He came to dinner, and he bought both you and Jake some lovely Birthday presents." "Of course, I do" replied Susy, "he was a really nice man." Well, he has offered me a job, most of which I could do at home. I would need to go into the office sometimes, but I could do that while you were at school, so I don't think it would affect you or Jake at all, and would bring in some money for us, what do you think?"

"You will still be able to collect me from school?" said Susy anxiously: she was still a bit nervous of walking home on her own, although Jake had done it a few times on his own. But Susy knew if he was supposed to walk her home, there was no guarantee he wouldn't go off and leave her. "No don't worry, if I did go into the office, I would do it in school hours so that I could still collect you." "In that case" said Susy smiling, "I think it is great idea, and you would be working with Peter who I am sure would be good to work with."

Then before Joyce could change her mind, she said in a rush, "and he has asked me to accompany

CHAPTER FOUR

him at a dinner dance at his house". "Are you going to go?" asked Susy.

"I am still thinking about it all" her Mum replied, "I think I will ring your Aunt Della and see what she thinks about me going back to work and out on a date with another man again, after all these years.

Her Mum went off to phone, and Susy sat and thought about all her Mum and said, then she had an idea, she went off to get Benny from his box. She said to him "I know you did not want us to tell Mum about you, but can you do something to help her make up her mind about a few decisions she has to make." "I can do something" said Benny "if you could get her to hold me in her hand, I might be able transfer some solutions to her." OK Susy replied, "I will try to do that."

Meanwhile, Joyce is speaking to her sister Della on the phone, she explains all that has happened, and asks her what she thinks. "I think you will have to be careful; you don't want this Peter to take advantage of you. Make sure he is going to pay you a reasonable salary, and that you have a contract that states about working at home plus the hours you are prepared to do. What about school holidays, what if he wants you to go into the office when the kids are off." Joyce sighed, "you are right I will need to talk to him again and get these points sorted out, and I am still not sure I can manage the work after all these years of being at home as a mother." "You are a clever woman" Della told her sister, "You will not have any trouble getting back into work" "As far as the night out is concerned, why shouldn't you go out and enjoy yourself, but again be careful he does not take advantage of you." "I do not think he is like that; I have only ever known him to be kind and gentlemanly."

"Well just take care "replied Della. "I was going to come and talk to you tomorrow, about a trip I am thinking of taking, so I might not be around when all this is happening." "Where are you going, and what are you going to do?" said Joyce, not sounding too sure about the only one she could talk to and get support from, not being there. "I will tell you all tomorrow, now I must go as I have a meeting, which I must attend. Love you, bye." And she was gone before Joyce could say any more.

Susy was sitting waiting for her mum in the lounge. "Mum, you remember you gave us some nice new coins that you got from the bank the other day," "Of course" said her mother, "have a look at this shiny new penny," said Susy, pressing it into the palm of her hand.

Joyce suddenly felt like she was falling down a deep well and thought of Alice in Wonderland and the

CHAPTER FOUR

rabbit hole, she felt herself stop and saw herself in an office, which she recognised as her husband's old office at Bolden Computers. She was sitting at a nice new modern desk, with a computer and a phone on it. She saw a face she knew, it was Ted, who was Peter's Office Manager. He was now speaking to her. "Joyce, I do not know what we would have done without you in the last year, you have been so useful to the Company, and finding that chap from Accounts that was stealing money from us was a brilliant piece of work. Pete has asked me to increase your salary, and says to tell you, that if you need any time off for school holidays or if any of the kids are ill you just take it, and we will not even deduct any pay from you. Well done, Joyce."

Next, she saw herself sitting at a big dining table at Westernmere Manor, Peter was standing next to her, saying it was the best thing he had ever done marrying her, that he had never been so happy, he just loved the children as much as he loved her, and thought of them now as his own. She had been such a good partner in the business and excellent at arranging and hosting all the social functions that had been held over the years. He was also looking forward in a few years' time to retiring and then going travelling with her.

DO YOU WANT TO KNOW YOUR FUTURE?

The picture suddenly faded, and Joyce was back in the lounge with Susy, who was sitting with a big smile on her face. Joyce shook her head; "I don't know what just happened, but I think I got a message on what to do about the job I have been offered and what my future might hold."

Susy noticed her mum had dropped poor Benny, when faced with what could be her future. Susy picked him up and put him back in her mum's hand again.

Joyce heard a little voice in her head;

> *"Like the pure wings of a dove,*
>   *faint heart won't win true love.*
> *True friends for now will be just fine,*
>   *and then find real love in its own time.*
> *He will not be perfect in every way,*
>   *but things will get better day by day.*
> *It may not always feel like a thrill,*
>   *but all your dreams he could fulfil.*
> *Don't think yourself a fool to like his charms,*
>   *you can really belong in his loving arms.*
> *Believe in a future where love would be missed,*
>   *and all you want is to be loved and kissed,*
> *So, give your love and give your heart,*
>   *with marriage vows to never again part."*
> *You could have no money problems ever again,*
>   *and perhaps one day you will live with Peter*
>   *and the children in that big house.*

CHAPTER FOUR

Woosh – Joyce came too, that was weird she thought, but it is true I suppose, I should give it a chance and see what happens, but I will tell Peter that we must take this slowly and be sure that we are both doing the right thing.

CHAPTER FIVE

The following night, Joyce's sister came to visit. Della was tall and slim, with long hair and she had a good tan from often being outside in all weathers. They wanted to have a quiet talk together and as Susy and Jake were playing a board game (Monopoly, Jake's favourite, as he always won,) they would not be disturbed or overheard.

"So, what is this trip you are thinking of taking", asked Joyce. "You know I have been working for the' World Wildlife Fund' for the past 6 months, I'm not sure if you know what they do."

Della Explained:
- World Wildlife Fund (WWF) is the leading organisation in wildlife conservation and endangered species.

DO YOU WANT TO KNOW YOUR FUTURE?

- Their mission is to conserve nature and reduce the most pressing threats to the diversity of life on Earth.
- These include food, climate, freshwater, wildlife, forests, and oceans.

Della had always had a passion for all wildlife:

Likes dogs and cats and even rats,
　from goosy gander to a giant Panda,
Doves in their house, to a little grey mouse
Cows in pens, to big brown hens,
　pigs in a sty and all birds in the sky,
Lions and tigers and monkeys too,
　in fact everything else that lives in the zoo.
Fish in the lakes, and long green snakes,
　a big polar bear in his icy lair
Also of course, a goat a horse, and don't forget
　always relevant a wonderful Elephant.

"Anyway" said Della," I have been asked if I would like to go to China to study their wildlife, I have never been there, but I hear they have, Chinese Alligators, Tigers, Leopards, Asian Elephants, Chow dogs, Golden snub-nosed Monkeys, Sable and of course Pandas. It would be good to go there and see all these animals and see how they are treated.

Some of the people are really poor, and live on a diet of just rice, wheat dumplings or noodles and

CHAPTER FIVE

pancakes, and if they are lucky enough to live near a river, fish too. Those a little better off, now-a-days eat potatoes and Manitou (which is a fried dough bread.) Of course, as in a lot of countries there are some very rich people too.

Susy who had been keeping one ear open to hear what her Auntie Della was going to do, thought would she be alright going to China? There was only one thing to do, she needed Benny's help. She ran off to get him and then took him to Della, "look Auntie, I have a new really shiny penny, have a look at it", and she placed it in her hand.

With the usual whistle and bang, a hole/tunnel opened up and Della stared at a scene in China, she saw a man explaining what they eat (as well as the rice etc that Della knew about) We eat snake meat and snake soup (as we think they have medical benefits.) We eat frogs, known as field chicken and Bull Frogs, we eat turtles too, as good for longevity, and bat stew. We are known to eat Chow dogs (black ones are better fried, other colours are stewed. (These dogs are not called Chow, because they make good 'chow', as commonly supposed.) Sometimes we eat Pangolin, but it is limited meat and has claws and scales, but again thought to have medicinal properties.

They are very expensive at 200.00 US dollars a kilo (apparently, they taste terrible!) The Chinese also keep pets of dogs, cats and rabbits, which they then later eat. One thing they never eat is Pandas. The culling of dogs used to take place (it was said to eradicate rabies) but it has now been outlawed, thanks to heavy fines and even prison.

Then Della saw herself coming back from China, feeling extremely sick with a high temperature, within a few weeks there was a full-scale Country alert that was a warning of a virus that came from China, not known if it was manufactured in a lab there, or caused from their diet of animals that carry diseases, like the bats and dogs.

With a flash the scene was gone. Della was horrified, she could not believe the cruelty and the diet they had (being a vegetarian herself, just the thought of the types of meat they ate made her feel sick.) And what about this virus, she could have bought this back to England and infected anyone she met and her family, it was unbearable to think about.

She was amazed that Joyce did not appear to have noticed that anything had happened, she was talking to the children, telling them to go and wash their hands and clean their teeth ready for bed.

Della said to Joyce "you know I don't think I want to go to China; I have been offered India and Brazil as well, I think Brazil would be better to help."

CHAPTER FIVE

> - **BRAZIL** – largest country in South America, they have a terrible drought this year, the worst spell in 91 years.
> - Largest Biodiversity in the world, they have over 3000 species of Fresh Water Fish, 70,000 insects and 55,000 different plants, and many species of animal, including Three-toed Sloth, Golden Lion Tamarin Monkey, Jaguar, Poison dart Frog, Carpybara (the largest rodent alive,) piranha, Toucan, Caiman (type of crocodile.) Anteater, and Armadillo.

So don't you agree this would be the place for me to go?" said Della. "I don't know much about any of these counties", advised Joyce," but if you must go, then I think you are right, Brazil sounds better than China, not that I want you to go at all, but I know you have to do what you want to do."

After Della left, Susy went to pick up Benny, "I am not sure quite what you have done, or how you did it, but I think me, and all my family seem so much happier and sure of what they want since you came into our lives. Thank you so much."

"It was a pleasure to help such a lovely family. I am still not sure I know exactly how I do it, but I am learning more about it as I go along."

Joyce was sitting on her bed, in her lilac decorated bedroom. She was pleased with the wallpaper she chose last year, and the pretty quilt cover and curtains that went so well with it. She thought about what had happened in the last few weeks and how things had suddenly changed. Jake seemed to be a much nicer little boy; she had been worried that he was turning into a person that no one would like. However, even yesterday he had for the first time let Susy win at Monopoly, she was delighted, and he had smiled at her. Also, after he had been advised about her job offer, and her chance to go out for an evening, instead of his usual sulking and saying she should stay with them, he had surprised her by saying that she should take the job and that she should go out more and that he and Susy would be alright with the babysitter, and if she could not collect Susy any time from school, he promised he would look after her and see her home without leaving her. This had made Joyce so happy she had nearly cried. She felt better now for the first time since the death of Norman.

Two days later, after her and the children had got home from school, she told them she had a surprise for them. "Come into the kitchen and look on the table" she said, nodding her head in that direction. Jake and Susy were so excited, they nearly fell over

CHAPTER FIVE

each other rushing to see what the surprise was. When they arrived in the kitchen, Jake stopped and stood open mouthed in amazement, there on the table was the train set that he had seen in the toy shop window, that he had so wanted. Susy also could not believe her eyes, there was the same pair of roller-skates that all her friends had, and she thought she would never have, but wanted so much. "Oh mum," they both cried, "thank you, thank you" Their Mother said, "you have both been so brave, losing your father, us not having much money, and both been so good lately that now I have a job (I am going to take Peter's offer) and will have money coming in again, I wanted you both to have a reward. My own reward will be that I will also say yes to the invite to the dinner dance he has asked me to," she smiled her face lighting up at the thought of it.

Later that evening, when the children were alone, they took Benny out of his box and told him about their wonderful surprise gifts. Benny said, "you both learnt some lessons, and both did not take the wrong path after learning what the future could be. Perhaps you can now see that being good has its own reward." "Yes, thanks to you" said Jake, "I am so glad I did not take that money from mum" "and I am glad I am not a bully" said Susy proudly, "we both want Dad to be proud of us." "I am sure, when he looks down on you, he will be," said Benny.

"I now want to tell you that my job is done," said the Benny, "I just have the feeling I now have to move on and see if I can help other people make their correct choices." "I don't want you to go" said Susy," neither do I" said Jake, but then they both said together, "but you must also do what is right."

"How do we decide who you should move on to?", asked Jake. "Well" said Benny "do you know of another family that may be having problems?" "Well, there is Percy my friend, him and his family are always shouting at each other and arguing. Percy has taken to eating far too much and just wants more and more food." Jake laughed and said "he will go pop soon; with the amount of pop, he drinks too. Ha Ha!"

"Well, it does sound as if there is a problem in that family, perhaps you can pass me on to one of them? Do you think Percy could keep a secret if I spoke to him?" "I should think he can," replied Susy gruffly, I have heard he keeps them all the time from his parents, and also about how many sweets and biscuits he eats." "He is coming to tea tomorrow, with his mum," advised Jake "so I can get you to him then."

CHAPTER SIX

It was the next afternoon; when Joyce and Mrs Sutton; Percy's mother, were sitting having a cup of tea and a chat. "Guess what Jill?" said Joyce, "I am going back to work, at Norman's old company, and I can work at home and do hours to suit the children's needs. Do have another cake, I bought these specially to celebrate." I'll have another one" said Percy greedily, who had already eaten two and had taken three of the biscuits off the other plate. "Don't be so rude said his mother, just go over there and play with Susy and Jake. "That is good news" said Jill, "when Percy is a bit older, I might like to find myself a nice part-time job, but at the moment as Percy is an only child, I think he needs all my attention." Joyce nodded but not very enthusiastically, as she actually thought Percy was very spoilt.

DO YOU WANT TO KNOW YOUR FUTURE?

Percy, Susy, and Jake were playing a game of cards, they were an old pack of Joyce's parents, that their grandmother had given them, not long before she died. The game was called 'Old Maid'.

- **OLD MAID** is an old card game from Victorian times, there are lots of illustrated colourful cards a pair of each character matching, plus just a single 'old maid' card, usually showing a grumpy looking old spinster woman.
- In Germany, the game is called 'schwarzer Peter' (black Peter) and in France it is called 'vieux garcon' (old boy.)
- The game is played by firstly shuffling the cards, then dealt out evenly between each player, face down on the table. The players pick them up and look at their own cards, making sure the others do not see them, if they already have a matching pair, they take them out and lay them on the table in front of them. They will then have less cards. (One player of course will have the 'Old Maid' card.
- The players fan out their cards and one player picks one card (draws without looking) from another player). When he has looked at it, without the others seeing, he checks if it matches any of the cards in his hand, if it does, he puts them both down on the table, if it does not match, he will put it into his own hand.
- It is now another players turn. If the player picks the 'Old Maid' card from the fanned-out cards of the other player, he must try and keep a straight face and quietly put it into his own hand, in the hope the next player will take it from them.

CHAPTER SIX

> - The pairs will eventually all match up and the loser is the person still holding the 'Old Maid' card. The other players will then usually point at them and shout at them Old Maid, Old Maid.
> - This game includes an element of bluffing. It can be played with a normal pack of playing cards, using the Joker as the Old Maid card.

The three children had just come to the end of a game and poor Susy was being shouted at by the other two as "Old Maid, Old Maid". Percy spoke to Susy, "as you lost you should go and get me some more biscuits" he said. "Don't you think you have had enough, you are getting quite fat," which was very blunt for Susy. "I am not fat" said Percy, "my mum says that I am just big boned," he tossed his head, which caused his (rather long) blonde hair to get in his eyes. Meanwhile, Jake had snuck off to go and get Benny in his box. "Instead of a biscuit, how would you like a magic penny?" asked Jake. Percy looked at the penny in the box. "It does not look much. If it has any magic abilities, what is it supposed to do? Do you have more of them?" said greedy Percy. Susy said, "you can keep the box as well, as it is his home, and by the way his name is Benny."

"Perhaps I can make a wish" said Percy, "ever since I visited the *Kents Cavern and *Cheddar

DO YOU WANT TO KNOW YOUR FUTURE?

Gorge with Mum & Dad I have wanted to go cave exploring and go pot holing. It could let me do that, because Mum says I can't until I am older."

This information came into the children's head:

- ***KENTS CAVERN PREHISTORIC CAVES**, is a cave system in Torquay, South Devon, notable for its archaeological and geological features.
- The prehistoric cave system is open to the public and has been a site of interest since 1952 and a scheduled ancient monument since 1957.
- Many people are surprised at the sheer size of the caves and just how much there is to see, with an extensive labyrinth of caverns.
- The caverns are one of the most important Stone Age sites in Europe and goes back to a time when caves were the home to ancient humans sheltering from the extreme weather, making fires, shaping tools and hunting the Ice Age animals.

- ***CHEDDAR GORGE** is a limestone gorge in the Mendip Hills, near the village of Cheddar, Somerset.
- The caves are where Britton's oldest complete human skeleton (estimated to be 9,000 years old) was found in 1903.
- You can climb hundreds of feet up or climb hundreds of feet down deep into the caves, where you can see magnificent stalactites and stalagmites.

- **CAVE SEARCHING**, also known as potholing, or spelunking in the USA, is the recreational pastime of exploring wild cave

CHAPTER SIX

systems. Caves formed by the weathering of rock often extend deep underground. It can be very dangerous and full training is required, also checking on all Health & Safety aspects and ensuring you have the right equipment.

- **DEEPEST CAVE SYSTEMS:** The deepest in the world is the Veryovking Caves at 2,212 metres and the Krubera Caves at 2,197 metres, both in Georgia, the deepest in the UK are Ogof ffynnon Ddu in Wales at 274.5 metres

'Oh, I remember leaning about stalactites and stalagmites at school" said Susy, "they are like big, long icicles, but you must remember which stand up from the ground and which ones hang from the ceiling, our teacher said remember mites grow up and tites come down," giggled Susy as she put her hand over her mouth.

"Just take the penny in your hand" advised Jake, "and see what it can do"

The message came through from Benny the Penny:

> *Should have been called Percy Pig, not Percy Sutton,*
>   *as he really was an awful glutton.*
> *Bring me biscuits, cakes and a pie, you would often*
>   *hear him cry, more sausage, bacon can you fry.*
> *Meat and Potatoes he would swallow,*
>   *sweets and puddings they would follow,*
> *Percy, he got round and fat, no one could dispute this fact.*

His overeating was not smart,
　　with danger to his poor old heart,
He really could not help himself,
　　or to try and redeem himself,
One day he would choke and catch his breath,
　　and it could all end in an awful death.

Percy gripped the penny tighter, his face turned red, when with a whoosh & a whistle, a hole and tunnel appeared, and he could not help but investigate it. He saw an older version of himself, but even fatter than he was now. He was in a cave system which, he had been exploring with some other people, but had been left behind because he could not keep up and was huffing and puffing. He was suddenly afraid he had got lost. The tunnel he was in suddenly got narrower and narrower, he got to a junction in the tunnel and went to go through, but he found he was stuck and could not move. He tried to push himself forward, but did not move, then he tried to pull himself backwards, but that did not work either, he was completely stuck. Percy started to yell for help, but nobody came, he shouted and shouted until he hardly had any voice left. He was beginning to despair and saying to himself if only I did not eat so much and get so fat, this would not have happened. When he thought he heard a noise. Oh no! he thought, I hope this tunnel does not flood! Just then round the bend came the group of people that he was with earlier. One of them had a

CHAPTER SIX

small pick and between them they managed to get Percy free. He was so embarrassed by it all, but at least he was thankful that he was free.

Whoosh! the hole disappeared as quickly as it had appeared to him. Percy was shaking, he looked around him, but of course there was nothing to see now.

"Tell us what you saw", both Susy and Jake said together, "I can't" stammered Percy, "it was too awful, but I will tell you I will never overeat again and I'll exercise more, I shall cut out sweets, biscuits, pies, crisps and all the other fattening things I have been eating." "It will be alright to eat them sometimes" said Jake, " just not too much or too often." Susy nodded her head in agreement.

"Whatever you saw," stated Susy, "it must have been the same sort of advice that both Jake and I received, so you see Benny really does work."

After his friends had gone home, Percy looked at Benny and thought I would have got even fatter and got into even more scrapes, if I had not had a look into the future, he really is magic.

Percy was about to put Benny back in his box, then he thought about his parents, although he was sure they loved him and his mum spoilt him, they did spend a lot of time arguing, and often stormed off when they lost their tempers. They could not agree on things, therefore leaving him alone. He had heard his mother complaining to his father about how much he was spending gambling and going to somewhere called a casino. His father had been complaining to his mother about her driving, how fast she dashed about and how many times she had hit or scraped the car.

I wonder if Benny can help them, like he helped Jake's mother he thought. I will try it on Mum first. He ran into the kitchen, which he had noticed his mum had been neglecting recently, it could do with a good clean and even some repainting.

Before Percy could speak, his mother said "what do you want for your tea, you could have burger and chips, followed by syrup pudding if you like?" His mother looked struck dumb, when Percy said, "do we have any salad, or if not some plain fish with new potatoes and I will just have a low-fat yogurt afterwards."

"I will see what I can do" stammered his mother, thinking to herself, that Percy must be feeling unwell.

"Mum" Percy spoke quietly to her, "I want you to look at this new shiny penny and hold it in your hand for me." "Well, I don't have much time, I must make you the meal you want and then I must dash off, I have to get on the motorway into town, and Eastenbrook gets remarkably busy this time of day. However, you have been a good boy, so I will do what you want." Mrs Sutton took the penny from Percy's hand.

CHAPTER SEVEN

Mrs Sutton suddenly felt dizzy, then she heard a little voice;

> "To this warning you must heed,
>   and really cut down that awful speed,
> If you keep going so very fast,
>   there is no guarantee how long you'll last.
> Into something you will bash,
>   and you might not even survive the crash.
> You are a mother and a wife,
>   so do not risk your precious life.
> So do not do this dreadful deed, think carefully
>   and cut down your speed."

DO YOU WANT TO KNOW YOUR FUTURE?

Mrs Sutton could not believe it when a hole/passage opened up in front of her, "Jill Sutton you must look in to see your possible fate" the voice told her. She cautiously came forward and looked into the hole – she could not believe her eyes, she was looking onto a busy motorway, she was driving her car and rushing along doing 85 miles an hour. Suddenly a lorry in front of her braked and swerved. Because of the speed she was doing, she could not brake fast enough, and went crashing into the back of the lorry. The last thing she saw was something falling off the lorry onto the top of her car, and the last thing she felt was a terrific bang as another car went into the back of her. Jill closed her eyes she could not bear to see any more.

When she did open her eyes again the traffic was at a standstill, but the road was crowded with police cars, ambulances and fire engines, and people dashing about. She heard a fireman say, I am not sure she will have survived, the car is squashed so badly, but we are getting the cutting equipment now to get her out as quickly as possible. Jill heard the terrible noise of them cutting metal, and then men trying to lift her through the side of the car, she tried to cry out with the pain, but no sound would come out of her mouth, and she passed out again.

When she next awoke, she was in a hospital bed, all wired up with drips and equipment that was bleeping all the time. She found she could not move

CHAPTER SEVEN

her head as it was held in a brace, and that both her legs were in plaster. Jill had worked in a hospital before she got married, so she knew that she was in a very bad state. A doctor arrived at her bedside and spoke to her "Mrs Sutton you are incredibly lucky to be alive, you hit that lorry at speed and a lot of large blocks of concrete came off the lorry and onto your car. 5 inches further over and you could have lost your head, but you still have bad concussion. Both legs were broken in 3 places, so I am afraid you will not walk again for some time. You will have neck problems later and you have 2 cracked ribs, but as I said it could have been worse, you could have lost your life. You will recover in time, but you will need a lot of nursing.

The hole shut down and everything went back to normal, but Jill just sat there. She started to cry with the shock, but she was a strong woman, and she pulled herself together, ran her hands through her long blonde hair. and took a deep breath.

I am not going to let that happen to me, I could have easily died and then I would have left Percy with no mother and Brian with no wife, or nearly as bad I could have been nothing more than a vegetable and not been able to do anything for myself. I could have been crippled and they would have had to push me around in a wheelchair, that is not what I want for my life. The doctors and nurses were marvellous , they worked so hard and they really cared about their patients. Jill smiled she had an idea. I can make amends for how stupid I have been. I know I will never speed or drive dangerously again, but I could go back to nursing, even part time while Percy is young. I am no Florence Nightingale, but nursing is such an old worthwhile profession.

- **FLORENCE NIGHTINGALE:** An English woman and founder of modern nursing and social reforms. Born in May 1820 in Florence, Italy and educated at Kings College, London.
- She came to prominence while serving as a Manager and trainer of nurses during the Crimea War, (1853 to 1856) looking after wounded soldiers in Constantinople (todays Istanbul.)
- She was known as the 'Lady with the Lamp' as she would walk among the beds checking on her patients, with the lamp held high and checking on their wounds and injuries.
- She had strong opinions on the importance of sanitation and cleanliness. She believed nursing was a spiritual calling and she could help patients with their health and spiritual distress.
- Miss Florence Nightingale would be impressed by the skills and experience of nurses today in providing safe and effective care.
- She died from Heart Failure on the 13 August 1910, at the age of 90 in Mayfair, London and is buried at St. Margaret's of Antioch churchyard.

CHAPTER SEVEN

Jill Sutton was now inspired to improve her life as she was only 34, plenty of time to make some changes, but where did all this come from? How did she get the flash of her possible future, then she remembered the penny Percy had given her, she saw it was now sitting on the table next to her; no, she thought that could not possibly have anything to do with it, but she must give it back to Percy.

Having seen the mess in the kitchen she thought to herself that is another change I must make. Instead of dashing out all the time she would spend time in the house tidying, cleaning and she would try to get herself a job nursing. She would contact an old friend of hers – Alison who may help her find a job, then she would have a little money to help with some home improvements, because her husband Sid didn't. He spent all his money on himself, mostly gambling it away. Jill now felt lighter, like she was as free as a bird.

Percy then entered the room, "I thought you were going out Mum" he said. "I was" replied his mother, "but I have changed my mind, I might get on with some housework instead" Percy tried not to show his surprise. "By the way Percy I have that penny you showed me, here you can have it back now." Percy looked at her strangely, had the penny, or should he say Benny, done anything for her.

She certainly seemed to be behaving differently; perhaps he would find out later.

His cat Betty watched sleepily from her basket in the corner of the room. He wondered if she knew about all these secrets and strange things that were going on in their lives.

Percy went out into the garden, he still had Benny in his hand, the only sounds he could hear was the traffic on the other side of the row of houses and an aeroplane passing overhead. He sat on the garden bench, which was a bit old and rickety and therefore groaned under his weight, he had not thought about it before, but he made up his mind to ensure that he did not overeat again, and he really must get more exercise. He would ride his bike more and perhaps the people next door might let him take their dog for a long walk. They were getting old now and could not take him far.

A little voice then spoke to him, "you really have learnt your lesson Percy and are now thinking all of the right things to do" "I am pleased with myself, and I think I may have helped mum too." "Yes, I believe you have," said Benny. "I do not know what I can do" sighed Percy "to help my Dad. He will not listen to anybody, and I have heard mum and

CHAPTER SEVEN

other family members giving him advice, but he never listens" "How would you be able to help him, I don't suppose he would even take you in his hand, the only money he would be interested in, is large notes".

"I have an idea" said Benny," you told me your father is a gambling man, why don't you bet him, that he cannot hold me in his hand for more than 2 minutes, which should then give me time to do what I can for him."

CHAPTER EIGHT

Percy's father, Sid Sutton, dressed in a good but old suit and flashy tie, sat in the kitchen, on one of the hard chairs at the table. It would not be something he would normally notice, especially as he had a lot on his mind, but he saw that the kitchen had been tidied and cleaned within an inch of its life. Jill must have been having a spring clean? He went back to his own thoughts, if only he could go to somewhere he often dreamt about:

- **THE LARGEST CASINO** in the USA, called WinStar World Casino and resort in Thackerville, Oklahoma. Open 24 hours per day.
- It had a mile of gaming floors, nine gaming plazas, electronic table games, the largest collection of casino games on the planet.

DO YOU WANT TO KNOW YOUR FUTURE?

- It has VIP ultra-high stakes, Poker tournaments and lots of slot machines.
- One lucky patron had bet one dollar and had won a jackpot of $569,981.84

What Sid would give to win that amount of money at this time! All Sid played was games of cards and roulette at a private gaming club he belonged to, and his luck seemed to have deserted him recently. He owed them so much money, he was frightened to go back there. He knew they had a reputation of dealing harshly with people who owed them money. It did not stop him itching to be betting on something, he just needed some stake money, however, he knew no one would lend him any more money, not even family or friends. He thought of Jill's friend Joyce Hill, she had some luck, she was now dating that rich chap from Westernmere Manor, her money problems were probably over, and it would not hurt to try and see if she could loan him a little money.

Just then Percy came into the kitchen, his dad looked at him and thought that he seemed different, he had certainly lost a bit of weight (still had a bit to go though) but he also seemed happier in himself.

"Hi Dad called out Percy, "I know how much you like to bet on things; I have a bet for you, I bet you cannot hold this little penny in your hand for 2 minutes, without letting it go." "Don't be silly", said

CHAPTER EIGHT

Sid, that would be no trouble at all." "Well go on then, to let's see you do it." "Give it here then," said his Dad. Percy tipped Benny from his hand into his fathers'. His father went rigid, as he looked at a black hole and tunnel which appeared right in their kitchen, and a voice spoke to him:

"You bet on anything at all, horses, dogs,
  flies up a wall,
Boxing, football and other games,
  even in a bingo hall.
All the lottery games and each scratch card.
To stop that now would be extremely hard.
You have always lost more than you have won,
  so now it has become a lot less fun.
As all of this could be predicted, as a constant
  gambler you are addicted. Now you are in lots of
  trouble, any more gambling it could be double."

"Look inside the hole and tunnel for you to see your possible fate", said the voice. Sid thought he might run away. Did he really want to know his fate? He bet it could not be that bad!

Wow! He peered in and saw himself walking in town. Suddenly, three men jumped out at him and dragged him into an alleyway. Another man that Sid recognised stood smoking a large cigar, "well if it is not my old friend Sid Sutton. "Ah hello Mr Curtis, how are you doing?" said Sid in a rather shaky voice. "All the better if you pay me the money you owe me, plus of course all the interest that is now due." Sid studied the tall tough man, who was wearing a most unusual shirt in two tones of green, looks a bit like a watermelon, thought Sid, but the look on Joe Curtis made him think he would not make that comment. He also could not lie to him. "I just don't have it Mr Curtis, not at the moment, but I have had an idea how to get some, if you could just give me another week."

"Well, I am in a good mood at the moment, so I will give you 5 more days to get all the money, but as a little example of what you might expect if you abuse my generosity and don't pay, my boys will give you a taste of it."

Sid looked horrified at what he saw next, he was lying on the ground, with his best suit (well his only suit actually) all torn and dirty, he had a cut along his cheek and a black eye, and by the way he was holding his stomach, probably a few broken ribs. The scene then changed rapidly, he was in his house and there were men taking out the furniture, his wife and son were crying, Jill sobbed "how could you do this. You borrowed money you could not pay back, and even some from our friends. You have gambled away the house and you sold everything of value that we own. Percy and I would now be on the streets, if my mother had not offered to take us in. We never want to see you again."

CHAPTER EIGHT

Sid held his head in his hands but when he looked up, he was back in the kitchen. I can't bear to lose my family and my home he thought, I have to try and make sure that none of this happens. He looked upwards towards heaven and made a solemn promise to never gamble again. I will not dream of all those places I want to visit to gamble. I will get a job, even if means working day and night to pay off my debts. I will also look after my family more. Sid suddenly thought about how he had seen this future that could happen to him. How on earth did that come about? Then he remembered it was just after Percy gave him that penny to hold. Was it some sort of magic? but he did not believe in magic – did he?

Sid sat at his kitchen table with his wife Jill and his son Percy. He looked very serious, but his gaze kept creeping round the room looking at the floor, ceiling and the table, anywhere except those sitting with him, then he made a serious effort and looked at them both. " I want to say first" he said in a very quiet voice "that I am sorry for all I have put this family though, and for not providing enough money for us to have a comfortable life. I promise I will make it up to you. I will work every hour to make more money, we will have the house decorated and some new furniture and perhaps later a holiday." Mrs Sutton looked at him strangely at first, her eyebrows raised, then she said, "is this really true Sid. Have you given up all the gambling and spending all your money on just yourself?" "I have darling" he replied, "I have seen what awful things can happen if I carry on the way I have been." (Percy smiled to himself, good old Benny has carried out his magic again.) " I am so pleased" said his wife crying and smiling at the same time. "Will you really keep your promise and will you stop gambling all together. I know it will be difficult for you."

"I am certainly going to try, and I bet you I will succeed", he then looked puzzled when his wife and son burst out laughing and then he realised what he had said, and he joined in with the laughter.

CHAPTER NINE

The rain had stopped again, so Susy and Jake had decided to play outside. They invited Percy to join them. (Now that he had lost some weight, they thought he could run around with them, and even keep up.) They went to their local park, which looked very beautiful in the Autumn sun and the leaves all golden, yellow, orange and brown. The children had a go on the swings, the slide and the climbing frame and then had a game of chase. When they were all worn out, they sat on a bench to rest. "I mustn't get my new jeans too dirty" said Percy," or I might get into trouble with my Dad." "I am pleased Benny was able to help your Dad," said Jake "that is both our families that have been helped by him. Is there anyone else we can think of that could do with Benny's help?" asked Susy thoughtfully. They all pondered the question.

"There is one person I can think of" said Percy, "my Mum's brother Arthur, Uncle Arthur Dooley, she was only saying the other day that she was worried about him. He was a boxer in his young days, but although he is older now and should be too old for fighting, he cannot stop. He picks fights with anyone he can, sometimes he hurts the other person, but often as not he gets quite badly hurt himself. Why would he keep doing that?

"Only one way to find out if Benny can help him, is to go and see him. No time like the present" shouted Percy. "Let's go, I remember where he lives, and it is not far."

They arrived at the address that Percy had told them, Susy looked around a bit apprehensively, it was a bit of a rough area, a lot of the houses needed a coat of paint, gutters replaced, and windows mended. Some had a lot of rubbish in the front, instead of a nice garden. There were old prams, washing machines, bicycles and rolls of old carpet etc.

Percy stopped at number 96 Granville Street. Susy was somewhat pleased to see it didn't have rubbish in the front, although the garden could have done with some work and the door could have done with a new coat of navy paint, it was not as bad as some she had seen.

CHAPTER NINE

Percy rang the doorbell, and the door was opened by a short but stocky man, the tops of his arms under his thin t-shirt could be seen bulging and stretching the material. He had a mop of what obviously had once been a blonde colour hair but now looked a dirty blonde with streaks of grey through it, and what appeared to be a blue bruise under his left eye.

"Hello my boy" said Arthur in his deep but cheerful voice to Percy. "What are you doing here, and who are your two little friends?" Percy did the introductions and said they were just passing and as he had not seen his uncle for a while, thought he would drop in and see him. Arthur looked a bit sceptical but opened the door wider and said "pleased to see you all, come in and let me get you some orange squash to drink - unless you would like something stronger" he said with a smile and a wink.

After the three of them had sat down together, with their glasses of squash, on the large leather settee, with Arthur sitting opposite them in a big rather saggy armchair, Percy thought he had better start the conversation and said, " my friends Susy and Jake would love to hear some of your boxing stories Uncle Arthur." At the same time Percy was slipping the box with Benny in, out of his pocket.

DO YOU WANT TO KNOW YOUR FUTURE?

As usual a rhyme came into everyone's head;

Boxing in a controlled way in a proper ring,
  might be alright to do your own thing,
However, street fighting or in a secret venue,
  would not be the best thing on the menu.
A hit in the eye, or in the stomach a hard punch,
  would put you right off your lunch.
You always like to punch and kick and then push
  and grab someone real quick.
You like to fight with all your might,
  any time of the day or night.
It may pay well and bring you a large purse,
  but at the end of the day would be a curse.
Your health would suffer whether you win or lose,
  it's up to you to decide what to choose.
These are not fair fights, they kick and bite,
  there is lots of trouble and the pain is double.

- **BOXING** – Boxing evolved between 16th – 18th century. The first newspaper report of a boxing match in England was in 1681. These prize fighters were the forerunners to modern boxing in the mid-19th century.
- Bare-knuckle boxing (or fisticuffs, as it was known) was popular in this time (this was boxing/fighting without the use of glove or other padding on their hands.) There were some rules, like not striking your opponent while he was down, but not much else.

CHAPTER NINE

- The first bare-knuckle champion of England was a James Figg, who claimed the title in 1719.
- A famous boxer Irish/ American bare—knuckle fighter John L Sullivan is recorded on an early photo posing in his fighting stance.
- Jem Mace is listed as the longest professional fighter in history – he fought for 35 years into his 60s and his las fight was recorded in 1909 age 78.
- Later there were many weight classes from heavyweight – 16 stone and over, middleweight – 14 stone, lightweight – 12.5 stone and flyweight 11 stone and under. For these titles to be held, all fighters were expected to give 100% effort and behave with complete sportsmanship.
- In modern times Boxing is a combat sport with 2 people wearing boxing gloves and other protective equipment, such as hand wraps, mouthguards and head gear when in training. They then throw punches at each other for a predetermined amount of time (called rounds) in a boxing ring, still following the rule of not hitting your opponent when they are down and stopping when a bell is rung.

While Arthur sat there looking a bit dazed, Susy slipped Benny into his hand. The usual whistle and bang came about, but Jake could not help but notice the light from the hole was dimmer than he had seen before, however, Arthur jumped up and looked straight into it. It felt like it lasted only a few seconds and also for a hundred years.

He saw an old barn that he recognised. It was 5

miles out of 'Westernmere. Men were gathering and parking their cars off the dirt road that led to the barn, round the back of it. Inside was lit by spotlights, pointing to an area in the centre of the barn covered in sawdust. Arthur saw himself standing there in his boxing shorts and boots, but no gloves, no mouthguard and certainly no head protection. Standing on the other side from him was his opponent dressed the same as him, but looking half his age, twice as fit and 10 inches (25.4 cms.) taller. Arthur knew he had the years of experience behind him, but he still felt nervous, which was unusual as he always loved to fight.

A horn sounded and his opponent stepped forward; Arthur stretched out his hand to shake, but all he got was a smirk and the opponent said, " I am Jason Temple – shouldn't take long for this fight to be over old man" and then he threw a punch straight into Arthur's chin. Arthur managed to block the next punch, but still didn't get to have his shot at him. Jason's next blow hit him hard on the side of his head and he went down on the ground, and he could not get up, he heard himself being counted out, but it sounded like he was under water. Jason Temple looked down on Arthur with a sad look on his face. "You really should give this up old man or someday someone is going to end up killing you – at least you don't have to worry about dying young."

Arthur heard what he said just before he passed out.

CHAPTER NINE

The Picture jumped to him being in a hospital bed with several doctors around him. "Mr Dooley" said one, " if you can understand me – how do you feel? The knock you had to the head caused you not only a bad concussion, but may have given you a bleed on the brain. We are going to give you a scan and do some more tests, however we are rather worried about you and what long term effects you may have."

Arthur suddenly came back to the kitchen, he swore and shouted, "what on earth was that? That certainly is not going to happen to me, I never lose a fight. What made me see all those scenes and what is this penny doing in my hand? He threw it across the room. The children were now quite frightened, "come on" said Jake, grabbing Susy by the hand and pushing Percy towards the door "let's get out of here before your uncle decides to hit one of us."

Once outside, they hurried down the road until they were a couple of streets away, then they stopped. "Well, that did not go well" said Percy, "Benny did not work his magic this time" "Oh no" wailed Susy, "we have left Benny behind, we have to go and get him" "I don't think that is a good idea" said Jake and Percy together. "We can't just abandon him, after all he has done for us" replied Susy beginning to cry. "That is true" said Jake, "but at the present time we need to let Percy's uncle calm down a bit, then perhaps we can ask him if we can look for Benny.

CHAPTER TEN

Poor Benny flew through the air, after being thrown by Arthur, he landed on the leather settee, but before he knew it, he slid down the side of the cushion. Benny was used to being in the dark of his own box, but he didn't like being in this dark unfamiliar place. He could still hear Arthur shouting and complaining to himself, but he could not hear the children's voices. I can't blame them for running away he thought, Arthur and his temper is rather frightening, perhaps they will come back for me later, but how are they going to find me?

Benny was sad that his magic help had not worked this time; he felt that his power seemed weaker than before. All Benny could hear was the tick of the old Grandfather clock, that seemed to go as slow as an old giant tortoise.

DO YOU WANT TO KNOW YOUR FUTURE?

As time went by Benny needed to occupy his mind. He remembered a book that Susy's mother was reading to her called 'Alice through the looking-glass' by Lewis Carroll, he had enjoyed the story and especially the nonsense rhyme in it, what was it called? Ah yes, The Jabberwocky it began;

> *"Twas brillig, and slithy toves*
> *Did gyre and gimble in the wabe;*
> *All mimsy were the borogoves,*
> *And mom raths out grabe*
> *Beware the Jabberwock, my son!*
> *The jaws that bite, the claws that catch!*
> *Beware the Jubjub bird, and shun*
> *The frumious Bandersnatch.*

It went on to say that the son had slain the Jabberwock, which secretly Benny thought was a shame.

I wonder if I could think of a good nonsense rhyme like that. After a little while he thought he had come up with a good start it began:

> *Wibble, wobble, double trouble, winky,*
>   *wonky, shifty, funky,*
> *Freely, peely, mousy, housey, winning, twinning,*
>   *how you're feeling?*
> *I want to dance among the stars,*
>   *walk on the sands below the seas*
> *To tiptoe on many mountain tops,*

CHAPTER TEN

To walk with tigers in the jungle and
On dessert sands doing bunny hops and
Fly with birds across the lands.
To talk to Llama's and eat in restaurants
in pyjamas.
To go up high on a garden swing and
end up on a kitey string.
Eat sugar mice and other things nice,
like crunchy carrots!
With chocolate parrots.
Run faster than a cheetah and
bow to the queen when you meet her.
Water ski the Artic, missing the polar bears,
which would be fair
And roller-skate round Trafalgar Square.

Whew, thought Benny I am exhausted after all that, I need to just lie here and have a rest. As he lay there, Benny heard voices, he hoped at first it was the children, but then he realised it was Arthur, he was talking to someone, but he was not shouting any more. He could not catch what they were talking about at first, he heard the word boxing, which made him worry. Then he heard the word help, so he wondered what was going on.

Arthur started to play some music, Benny found he liked listening to all the different tunes and the words to the songs, the radio seemed to be sending him a message. He heard one that he liked -from some beetles- beetles that sing? (Especially as it was called Penny Lane) and another sung by Louis Prima, called Pennies from Heaven. Slowly he drifted off to sleep.

Jake, Susy and Percy were in the park, it was a cold but bright day, with sunlight filtering through the clouds. The children were discussing what went wrong with the future telling for Arthur and poor lost Benny. They all felt dreadful about leaving him behind and not having the courage to go back to the house to get him. "Look" advised Percy, "it was my idea to go and see my uncle Arthur, even if I did just want to help him, so I will go back and see him, stand up to him if I have to." "No" replied Jake, "we went into this together, we found Benny originally before passing him to you, so we should go with you" "I agree" said Susy – "even if I am a bit afraid of your uncle."

As they left the park, a shower of rain started to come down, even though the sun was still shining; moments later a colourful rainbow appeared. "Oh look" cried Percy, "we should find the end of the rainbow to make us rich." Susy looking a little sad as she remembered something her father used to say – she told them "*You don't need to look for the end of the rainbow and for a crock of gold, the beautiful*

CHAPTER TEN

rainbow is enough". "Yes" said Jake, "I remember Dad saying that." "Nice saying" said Percy, "but can we get a move on, I am beginning to get rather wet."

They arrived at Granville Street and at Arthur's house. Susy was a bit surprised to see the front garden looked a little tidier than when they were last there, but she did not say anything because she was getting more nervous the nearer she got to the door. Percy seemed to hold his breath before ringing the doorbell, he heard footsteps coming to the door and felt like running away. Much to surprise of the three of them, Arthur opened the door to them with a big smile, just as he had the first time. "I wondered when you children would turn up again, you had better get in quick before you get soaked."

Arthur was looking much smarter than the last time they saw him, also the bruise he had was faded to a pale yellow, and there were no new ones.

"Sit down children I have something to tell you", said Arthur quite excitedly. Although the boys were listening and asking questions, Susy was not. She did not know why but she was suddenly drawn toward the leather settee and she could feel Benny close and calling for her. She slipped her hand down the side of the settee and felt around in the dust that was down there. Suddenly she felt the round shape and grasping at it, pulled her hand out and there was Benny. "Oh, I am so glad to see you" she cried, "and I am really pleased to see you too" whispered Benny in a small quiet voice. Just then the boys came to see what Susy was doing, they both shouted. "We are so glad that you have been found"

"I am just sorry that I let you down with Uncle Arthur" said Benny sadly. He was most surprised to see that both boys had beaming smiles on their faces.

"You didn't let us down" advised Jake, "Arthur has just been telling us that he thought long and hard about what he saw and realised that it could happen to him like that, he could end up like a cabbage if he carried on fighting. On the other hand, he did not know what he would do if he did not have boxing in his life. Then an idea came to him, he went down to the local boy's gym and offered his services as a trainer, that way he could show them the correct way of boxing (and not to do what he had done.) Apparently, they are really grateful for his help. He also thought that other improvements in his life were needed too, so you see it has been just as successful as your other future insights."

Susy clapped her hands in glee and nearly dropped Benny back down on the settee, which made everyone laugh. However, she sensed all was not right with Benny. "What is the matter" she asked, "is there anything we can do for you?"

CHAPTER TEN

Benny said, "I am getting weak, and my powers have nearly all gone, but while I was lying there, I received a sort of message of what I need to do, but I will need your help."

CHAPTER ELEVEN

Jake and Susy were in the kitchen with their mother. They kept looking at each other, as their mother was busy mixing a cake. "This is a Lemon Drizzle cake for tea on Sunday when Peter comes, it is his favourite." Jake nodded at Susy to start talking. "Mum, you told us that you and Peter are going to get married next year and that we are all going to move into his big house. Does that mean you are happy again now?" Joyce looked at her young daughter; "I know that you are thinking about your father, I loved him very much and I always will, but now I love Peter as well. He makes me happy, and he wants to look after me and both of you." "It is brilliant both Jake and I like Peter, and we are glad you are getting married."

Susy took a deep breath, "what Jake and I wanted

to talk to you about is how you came to be together and fall in love." Joyce looked puzzled, "darling I am not sure what you mean?"

Susy started from the beginning and told her mother everything that Benny had done to help her, Auntie Della, Percy, Percy's Mum, and Dad and finishing with his uncle. Joyce looked shocked but said "I can hardly believe it, and yet in some ways it makes sense. I remember that weird feeling I had, seeing something that might happen. What I don't understand is how the penny talks to you?" "Well," replied Susy "he of course can't actually talk, but we hear his voice in our heads, and he can understand what we are saying."

"I would say that it cannot really happen, but all the people you mentioned have had better lives in the past 6 months including me so it seems it must be. Where is your penny and why are you telling me about all this now?"

Jake now spoke up. "We need your help, or rather Benny does – that is what we call him. All the magic he has done has drained his power and he is weak. He needs now to go home." "Where is that and how do we get him there?" cried their mother. Jake said "it is alright he told us what is required. You remember the day you took us to the bank and later you gave us some coins that were new and shiny, well Benny was one of those coins. He now needs to go back to that bank and be given to the Manager

CHAPTER ELEVEN

– Mr Hodgson." "I can do that" said Joyce, "but what am I going to say to him, he will think I am mad." "Perhaps he won't" advised Jake. "You get Benny, and meanwhile overnight I will have a think about what I am going to say to him when we go to the bank tomorrow morning a think about what I am going to say to him".

Joyce was not convinced that Jake was right and that Mr Hodgson would not think she was mad or just making up stories. After all it did seem to be impossible, however, her children didn't lie not even Jake anymore. All those people had turned their lives around and made changes for the better, so she had better come up with a plausible tale about why she wanted to return just one penny to the bank!

The following morning looked much the same weather as when she took the children to the bank the last time. Rain clouds had gathered in the sky and the sun was missing, completely hidden away.

"Jake, Susy" she said "You had better put on your raincoats and your boots, I think we may get wet later on this morning." Jake did not look very happy about it but thought he could not complain as it was them who had asked their mum to take them to the bank. Susy on the other hand was delighted to be wearing her yellow raincoat with matching yellow boots that had pictures of red daisies on them. She had Benny in her hand and was just going to put him in his box, when she said to him, "I am going to be very sorry to say goodbye and see you go, I know we are doing the right thing. You deserve to be going home after everything you have done for us and other families, but I am going to miss you and I will never forget you." She gave Benny a kiss just like she had done once before. "Do you think we will ever see you again?" Benny's voice came into her head very softly – "You may well see me again young Susy, maybe in another form, but I will never forget you either, I am sure you are going to grow up to be a fine young lady and we will meet again someday."

Susy slipped Benny into his box and put it in her pocket, she felt sad, but also pleased about the last thing he had said.

The three of them walked to the bank, Joyce was thinking about what Peter had said the previous week about getting her, her own car. She had told him it was not necessary, but Peter had been quite insistent and on a day like today with the long walk and the weather looking to turn bad, perhaps it wouldn't be such a bad idea. She just didn't want to feel she was taking advantage of his money and position.

When they got near the bank, Joyce began to feel a little nervous, she had been thinking all night about what to say to Mr Hodgson and had not come up with anything that did not sound ridiculous. Mr Hodgson was a very nice man and

CHAPTER ELEVEN

always talked kindly to his customers, but she wondered if he still would to her after she told him what they had come for.

Joyce went to the Customer Service desk; she was pleased to see that an old school friend of hers was standing at the desk. "Hello Pauline, how are you today?" "I am fine" replied Pauline and how are you, I heard you got engaged to Peter Westbook, from Westernmere Manor, I am very pleased for you, you deserve to have a second chance at happiness." "Thank you" said Joyce, "can you possibly help me, I do not have an appointment, but I would really like to see Mr Hodgson this morning if possible." Pauline was a very efficient assistant to Mr Hodgson and would certainly protect him from people who she did not think ought to get into see him. "I will see what I can do, I will speak to Mr. Hodgson and if he can spare the time to see you. Wait over there on those chairs and I will find out. Oh! are these your children? My how they have grown since I last saw them, quite grown up looking." "Yes, they are mine and a credit to me, after the hard time they had after Norman died."

After a few minutes, Pauline came back and said with a smile "Mr Hodgson says he will see you now, he has a 20 minute gap before his next appointment; do you want me to watch the children while you go in and see him?" Joyce looked at the children, and they both shook their heads. "No it is alright they can come in with me." Pauline looked a bit surprised but ushered them into the Manager's office.

Joyce was again struck by the old-fashioned furniture and décor, but with some modern equipment including a computer. She remembered being told some time ago that the building, many years previously, was an Apothecary that made potions and lotions *(like a Pharmacy as it is known today).*

"Good morning, Mrs Hill, and good morning Jake and Susy." If Joyce had not been so nervous she might have wondered how he knew the children's names as she didn't remember ever having told him them. "What can I do for you today?" said the kindly old gentleman, Joyce stuttered " I, I have come about …" She did not know what to say next. Instead Susy spoke for her "It is about the penny we got from your bank, it was a very special penny, but now it has to come home and be returned to you." Mr Hodgson smiled. "Well that is different, most people want to take money out of the bank, they don't usually want to bring it back." "It is important that he comes back to you" said Jake, "so you must take him." "Him?" said Mr Hodgson, "that is curiouser and curiouser, I don't know why you want to return just one penny to me, but I will take it if you want me to." Joyce then had the courage to speak also, "I don't think you would believe me if I told

CHAPTER ELEVEN

you all the story behind this, but it is important that the penny comes back to the bank." Susy took the box out of her pocket, opened it, and lifted out Benny and handed to Mr Hodgson. "Thank you" he said, "I will take it".

Joyce wanted the embarrassment to end so she started to push the children towards the door, saying "Goodbye" over her shoulder. Susy turned to take one last look at Benny and mouthing Goodbye to him. Then Mr Hodgson winked at her and said very quietly, "Don't worry Susy I will look after Benny."

When they got outside the bank, Susy whispered to Jake, repeating what Mr Hodgson had said. "He must be part of Benny's magic as he knew his name and he is going to look after him, so I feel so much better about leaving him, although I will still miss him." "So will I" said Jake sadly, "but he did say we might see him again someday."

CHAPTER TWELVE

Rodney Hodgson sat back in his big old leather chair and put Benny on his desk in front of him. He took off his thick round glasses and rubbed his eyes. He took out of his top pocket a clean, white handkerchief to wipe the lenses, before putting them back on.

"That is a lovely name you were given – Benny, it suits you. What a nice family the Hills are, I think I made the right choice in giving you to them and they were lucky to get you. You helped a lot of people, and I am sure they are grateful, even if they do not really know how it happened. Your useful tips about the past were a nice touch, but what can I say about your poetry, awful, simply awful (he said with a big smile on his face) however, I am glad you managed to return home to me."

Benny answered in his tired quiet voice, "they were all nice families, but I was especially fond of Susy. We seemed to have a sort of connection, but I am also glad to get back to you. What is going to happen to me now?"

"I have to return you to the Royal Mint, London" replied Mr Hodgson, "I have a friend there that will make sure you are renewed, and your powers and strength will be restored. If I am lucky, you will be returned to me, but I am not sure if you will remember this past life, I do hope so." "So do I. I have enjoyed meeting and helping all these families and I would like to see them again, as well as perhaps meeting some new people to help. I promise to try and improve my poetry," said Benny with a little laugh in his voice.

Mr. Hodgson said, "there are certainly a lot of people who need help and guidance, in many different ways, so I hope you will be back to your full strength and powers soon."

"Well then" said Mr Hodgson, "let's get you packed up and sent back to the Royal Mint as soon as possible. I do hope we will see each other again in the future."

THE END - OR IS IT ??????

ABOUT THE AUTHOR

Having been born in the 50s, I remember when I first started work and the time when the country went to decimal currency, so I had to type invoices in both £ s d and new pounds and pence.

My background is all office work, which I have always enjoyed. I remember how pleased and proud I was when I got my Diploma in Management.

My last job before I retired was as a Practice Manager in a large Health Centre. It kept me very busy pleasing doctors, patients and staff.

I would like to give my thanks to my father (Albert, now 95 years old) who always encouraged me to be independent and to go for anything I want to do.

The same with my husband Jeremy who has encouraged me in writing this book and for putting up with me when I got frustrated with getting the plot right.

My thanks also go to my sister Della, friends Pauline and Chris and Avril who have done some proof reading for me,
I could not have achieved writing this book without the help of Alex Chapman my editor and Clare Baggaley (Reedsy) for her beautiful book cover and illustrations and her good advice.

JANET LAKE

Printed in Great Britain
by Amazon